The Art of Delegation

Focus on What YOU Love to Do!

John D. Curri II

Forward

As a young entrepreneur, I always felt a sense of power that was driving me forward. Over time, my sense of curiosity began to blossom; where discovering new things and wanting to learn and know EVERYTHING kept sucking me into books and activities that would shape my future.

One day, I woke up and realized I was wishing the days were a little longer, or the hours would just pass slower, so that I could catch up – or even maybe get ahead. The more I dove deeper into the complexities of my business(es), the more responsibility I was assuming, the less time I had.

Working MORE did not seem like the answer.

Ah, Delegation. Certainly not a new concept; however masterfully conquering the ART of Delegation was much more profitable than any other business acumen I could acquire.

Read that again… ***the most profitable activity I ever did, for my business and my family, was to learn the ART of Delegation.***

Without a grasp on the true nature and art of delegation, the days continued to become shorter, the time passed quicker, the market continued to become tougher, the competition was fierce and my margins decreased. I could not keep up!

Glass ceilings suddenly appeared, competition did "me" and "my concepts" more effectively, business and life became very challenging

My family was growing up around me. I missed events, I was late to parties, my "personality" suffered, I was tired and stressed, I missed special moments and I realized that there must be a "breaking point" for everything if you do not learn to delegate.

The ART of Delegation can be used in applications as simple as a family discovering how to get chores done during the week so they can play on the weekends; to a CEO and team figuring out how to put a rocket into space. Whether you are in sales, manufacturing, the service industry or running a household - this book is for you.

Is it easy? Well, it is not as hard as I was working before; that is for sure! I had to commit to the changes even when it was tough. I had to work on trusting the process; and identify the qualities in the people around me that were beneficial and those that were detrimental to the process.

When you learn the ART of Delegation, master it and put it into practice; your life and those around you will change for the better.

TABLE OF CONTENTS

ACKNOWLEDGMENTS

I wanted to shake things up with a new kind of training to help my team move past their "glass ceilings"; a new message and a different face.

I was introduced to Ellen Onieal through one of my team partners, Tim and Brittany Breil . After speaking to her, I hired her for a team meeting presentation at the end of 2022 on goal setting.

With a similar message to this book, I was proud of the message that she passed on to my team about focusing goal planning on daily activities, and inward reflection on why and how things get done more simply - a self-delegation or accountability of sorts.

After hearing this message, one of my goals was to get this book written. For me, for my team - it was time. I decided to collaborate with Ellen and delegated it to her to get it published.

The ART of Delegation

1 LISTEN

Ask Yourself these questions.

Are you ready to grow as a person?
Are you willing to leave ineffective habits behind?
Are you ready to create more freedom for yourself?
Are you ready for your business to grow?
Are you ready to make more money?

Listen.

I know you are thinking, everyone's parents had "that saying" that stuck. My childhood was no different.

My Dad would say **"You have got TWO ears and ONE mouth; Listen more and Talk less"** he would sternly say. Wise words from a smart family man who I admire for his tenacity, dedication, and love in everything he did.

Early in my career, and when I had the opportunity for the first time to manage people and processes, I would go into meetings, lunches, or discussions ready to "fire off a huge agenda" and tell everyone my thoughts, my feelings, my directions.

After many unsuccessful attempts of "reaching my team," I realized everyone really wanted to be heard; to talk about themselves, their issues at hand or problems, and they needed to talk and for someone to **listen**.

There is an ART of listening. Do you know the difference between Hearing and Listening?

Merriam-Webster defines **Hearing (passive)** as the "process, function, or power of perceiving sound; specifically: the special sense by which noises and tones are received as stimuli."

Listening, (Active) on the other hand, means "to pay attention to sound; to hear something with thoughtful attention; and to give consideration." It is not just hearing the sounds; it is an understanding of the sounds.

Here is what I have learned about the two. Just because someone hears what I am saying and may even acknowledge as such, does not mean that they listened.

Just because I heard...

- .. "The mission" does not mean I understood it.
- .. the words, does not mean I understand their context or meaning
- .. sound coming out of your mouth, does not mean I understand you (famous line in a movie, right?)

Studies have proven that there are listening styles with every Adult Learning Principle.

Active Listening – understanding the meaning and intent

Appreciative Listening –for music or poetry

Information Listening – listening with goal of learning

Reflective Listening – could be mirroring

Dialogic Listening – team deciphers the meaning

**I would encourage you to start identifying how people listen to you in different settings – What kind of listeners are they, what kind of listener are you? **

There will be tell-tale signs of what type of listener you are and what kind of listener your partner is. For instance:

Active Listener – takes notes, leans in

Appreciative Listener –body language clues (eyes closed)

Information Listening – taking notes or recording

Reflective Listening – sales technique of mirroring and repeating.

Finally, one not mentioned is the famous "**Listen to respond**" person. This person will interrupt your stories with their version of their story, and probably has not heard a thing you have said.

This chapter is about becoming a Better Listener.

What kind of listener are you?
How do you check for understanding?
Can listening "appropriately" be a "thing"?
Can I train people on how to be an effective listener?

I must become A Better Listener myself

"What are some things I need to understand about myself to be a better listener?"

Listening requires focus and I had to understand what my attention span was.

I needed to realize how <u>much</u> information was going to be directed at me, and what my capacity was for handling that amount of information. (Am I tired, hungry, distracted?)

I learned, as a Bonus, that if I asked better questions, I would become a better listener because I would be able to get to the pertinent information and not get a lot of "fluff" that may cloud my understanding.

Setting appropriate time for meetings/interactions that required my full attention was important to avoid distractions.

Understanding the scope of the information I was receiving (is someone just "telling me a story" or do I have to remember or act on any of this information)

Think about, as the listener, how many times you have been to a presentation where you needed to learn something. If you were too cold, or hungry, or bored, tired – how much did you comprehend? How much did you listen to?

My awareness? I have my own 'bad listening' tendencies. I get distracted just like the next person. However, I learned that I can become a better listener by just setting myself up for success.

- I interrupt less
- I understand more
- I appreciate the other person's vocabulary
- I learn new contexts or nomenclature

The benefits to becoming a better listener myself, is that it helps with understanding **how I communicate to others.**

8

The ART of Delegation is quite a process – and it is a technique that is profitable for both family and business situations.

Once I learned how important understanding listening styles and body language cues were...

- Instantly, my delegation techniques improved.
- I understood where my style of communication was lacking
- I was able to appreciate other terminology and language (and caught up on some pop culture!)
- My relationships improved because my understanding improved.
- I saw a change in others' "moods" around me – more because I think they understood me better, is that possible?

A few more important things about listening. I realized how important Body Language is. I know it seems like a simple thing to overlook; but once I really paid attention to my body language, I realized I did not always convey my sentiments correctly.

This is what I had to learn.

- Communicate Sincerity
- Make Eye Contact
- Acknowledge appropriately (ex: head nod)
- Avoid distractions (tapping, rocking, fidgeting)
- Reward, Thank, Appreciate
- Not seem "rushed"

The best teacher is experience. Involve yourself in conversations where you will have to be an active listener; especially in the situations where you are asked to do something.

- Pay attention to how people delegate to you.
- Pay attention to the delegating in your household; to your spouse or children.
- What was received well, done without incident?
- What produced the best results?

Arguably, not only does listening **enhance your ability to understand better and make you a better communicator**, it also makes the experience of speaking to you more enjoyable to other people.

Step ONE in the ART of Delegation…. In order

to be heard, I need to listen better.

ACTION ITEMS

I am going to add a few things to the end of each of these chapters that may entice you into perfecting each skill that we discuss (that you read).

The first goal is to practice listening. If you find yourself TALKING a lot. then you are **not** doing it right. The second goal would be to try and remember and recall the details of the conversation. I find that I will take notes that I feel may become important items for reference.

- **Attend a networking/social event.** Prior to going to the networking event, construct open ended questions - you know what those are, right? An open-ended question, simply, is one that there is not a YES or NO answer to. As your "audience" answers those questions, prepare follow up questions to learn more.

During the conversation, do your best not to contribute to the answer or the questions unless prompted to. Just listen - the only thing you should do is ask questions.

- **While in a conversation with someone, get a comfortable stance or sitting position that allows you to concentrate on the conversation and not get distracted by others, loud noises, or other interruptions.** Give your full attention to the other person's dialogue, including eye contacts and appropriate facial acknowledgement. Refrain from swaying or other distracting body language, looking away at watches, phones, clocks on the wall etc.

A few of my challenges:

…. when people speak very softly, I have a hard time understanding them - I have learned to pick up some "lip reading" skills as well as body language "tell tales".

…. I am relatively good with foreign accents and diction, but have been challenged with some dialects that are unfamiliar. I try to focus on the key words, and then repeat those to make sure I understand the main points of the conversation. This takes practice, and maybe a quieter spot in the room.

…. I am terrible with names. Name tags are a crutch

and helpful. When that is not prominent, I try to repeat their name during the conversation or introduce them to another person nearby.

…. I have been hooked into conversations that were not going as I had planned. Restroom breaks are always an easy "out," comfortable exit from a conversation.

…. I must practice "no judgment" when engaging in conversations that are inappropriate for me. Ironically, most times if I just practice good listening skills; I can understand others' points of view and my "judgment" becomes more "curiosity".

- What are some other assignments/practices can you do on a weekly basis to help you with your listening skills? What challenges do you face with listening?

- Remember that every challenge that you face with the ART of Delegation can be overcome with practice and diligence. Whether you become a great delegator, or not, depends on your mastering of these skills.

FACTS ABOUT LISTENING

- Listening is our primary communication activity
- Our Listening habits are not the result of training but, rather the lack of training
- Most Individuals are inefficient listeners
- Inefficient and Ineffective listening is extraordinarily costly
- Good Listening can be taught

A Quick Story:

I remember like it was yesterday. I was 9 years old. My parents were average working folks; another couple introduced them to the multi-level marketing business called "Amway". They had weekly meetings in our home and their friends' homes.

While the adults had their meetings, I was instructed to do something constructive; like read a book or watch TV in the other room. I was 'notorious' for eaves dropping, lurking in the doorway or hallways so I did not miss anything.

I was obsessed with learning all I could. I was totally consumed with knowing why so much time and effort was dedicated to selling toothpaste and laundry detergent. I needed to get the big picture.

My parents once bragged to me about a guy they met "Dexter Yager" that was a positive influence on their lives. I remember them telling me he had a nice "Million Dollar RV" and was top in sales all the time. I could hear the excitement in my dad's voice as he spoke about the success stories of other's and I was surrounded by the success my parents also experienced.

Around this time, I started understanding the concept of "selling", and through listening to the kitchen table talk, I got excited about selling "things"; I wanted to be successful like the people my dad was always telling me about.

One day my parents offered me $10 if I would read the book by Zig Ziglar's "See you at the Top". A little back story, my parents did not believe in "chores" for dollars – like a weekly allowance. The only way I could make extra money was for some kind of "Self-help" – read a book or take a class. Not a typical upbringing; however, they set me up for a robust and successful life.

As I wrote this book and reflect on what the 'forks in the road" were for me. I realized that listening, well more of the eaves dropping, was instrumental in my curiosity of success at a young age. It was a skill that I developed because of my curiosity.

Listening became something that may have had a sneaky connotation to it in the beginning; but as my skill developed, and my communication became better I realized what I would or could be missing out on.

Maybe I still eaves drop. It is all with the best intentions. Even now, I am still a very curious person.

2 IGNORE

Ask Yourself these questions.

**What sucks up your time without reward?
Are you willing to be real about your time?
Are you ready to create more freedom for
yourself?**

Hopefully you have come to realize that the true

ART of Delegation is getting in front of the mirror first, and shining the light on what we personally must change in order to delegate and manage people and life effectively.

For many, the IGNORE title of this chapter may come across as arrogant or disrespectful. What I found is that I had to start learning to IGNORE some things in life, in order to save room for the qualities that made my companies GREAT!

I am sure you have heard the phrase "Ignorance is bliss sometimes". I choose not to know. For instance, I never was engrossed in the latest fad of shows on TV or Cable provider; I never watched the sensational news of the O.J Simpson trial; or the latest by the Kardashian tribe – I am, and remain untouched by things that do not serve me.

With the movement of what I call "information overload" since my early thirties, I have done my best to filter out what is "IGNORABLE". I choose the notifications that infiltrate my phone and portable devices, inboxes, social media and the like.

You may be thinking, what does IGNORING have to do with the ART of Delegation? It sheds an infinite amount of light on what distracts people, in general, from getting things done.

I faintly chuckle when I hear myself saying, "just give me Five minutes, and I'll be done," knowing that email needs to be reread 14 more times, and I need to sit and wait to make sure that it was sent correctly; did not bounce back, etc. That five minute's is now fifteen, because while the email loaded, I got 3 text messages that "I had" to answer immediately; oh, and then there was that funny video…. you get my point.

Bottom line is, if you want to be a specialist in something great; if you want to have a great family that communicates well; if you want to have an organization that can count on you for direction; Identify the IGNORE's in your life.

IGNORE things:
- You have no control over
- That do not serve your purpose, mission, or Love
- That involve other people's drama

INSTEAD
- Set Boundaries
- Love Yourself
- Resolve issues quickly

- Set timers for selected activities

Personally speaking, I think the hardest career for distractions has got to be Social Media Manager or the like. Think about what they would have to do to ignore the pop up's, pinging and dinging, and decipher which ones are important and which should be ignored.

Ah, I got off track. This chapter is about understanding distractions that can be avoided. My personal distractions have been social media, alerts, apps, text messages. I have done things to prevent those distractions from happening, not by IGNORING, because I know they are still there; but by setting boundaries that make me more effective.

For instance, I do not leave social media on my phone anymore. Unfortunately, it can be for some of us, like a Twelve Step program to break this habit because of the Artificial Intelligence built in to make us addicted to those pings and dings.

I limit my TV, news and the like to certain times.

I have favorite news channels that contribute to my effectiveness for me to be able to access the information that I want without overload.

Here is a big one: Do not let other's poor planning become your emergency. This is a total energy sucker and it always results in the problem being bigger than it is. Breathe, take your time and think through every solution before acting. (Other's poor planning caused it; use your planning skills to fix it)

All in all, maybe this chapter should be called **CHOOSE, rather than IGNORE**. I got control of my time and distractions quickly by just paying attention to how much of those precious hours of the day are being dedicated to the activities that make me a better person, husband, father, manager, CEO and friend.

Step 2 in the ART of Delegation. **Ignore the things that do not serve you**. As a bonus, the people you are delegating to will not say things like "You looked busy, I didn't want to interrupt you", the whole purpose, after all of the ART of Delegation is to look **less** busy, to be **more** approachable, to allow more missions to be accomplished.

...moving on to chapter 3....

But first, let's make a checklist of things you can work on to get better at IGNORING the things that do not serve you.

- Complete a very simple "time study" on a typical day. What did you spend your time doing and how did it serve you?
  - Remembering, of course, that down time/relaxation time is important and can be a recharging of your day.
- Turn off ONE notification or Interruption per week. Social Media is an easy one. Subscriptions. Other non-essential "bings" "pings" or "tings"
- Set alarms for non-essential activities - completion times.
- Set alarms to test your "this will only take me five minutes" skills.

A few of my challenges:

… FOMO - fear of missing out.
…. I have several businesses; what happens if there is an emergency and I have turned off my notifications
…. staying vigilant with my time and activities that serve me

... I do not like to say NO. I had to learn how to manage that

Ignoring FACTS
... maybe not facts as much as questions to ask about the way you are spending time. As you are doing the "time study" as explained earlier, you can ask yourself some questions:

- Does this activity or interruption align with my goals
- What is the relationship with the "Requestor" of my time?
- Is it a Quality Request? (Something that is important, or you could rationalize that it is a quality request)
  - Does it fit on my priority list?

CAN THE REQUEST BE DELEGATED?
Some of you may be thinking - hey, that is a lot to go through to decide whether to ignore something or not. Think of how much time you will save by doing this prework.

A Quick Story:

One of the issues of always being curious, is that there is always a question to be answered. A thirst for knowledge can get overwhelming. Add the influx of cell phones, social media, notifications, shitty news reports that drained me.

I realized I had "Time Burglars." Mindless activities that had no positive impact on my life.

It took time to learn how to ignore what was not important. I did a simple time study here and there and realized those "things" that were depleting my time and successful opportunities.

To connect these first two chapters. I listened to everything. I would say, that I acted on what I heard, as well. The ignore portion of this was to "weed out" what was important. Trust me, until I learned what I needed to ignore, I always looked busy, unapproachable, and stressed.

"All of a sudden" life started taking a different shape. I was getting more things accomplished and opportunities started presenting themselves. My relationships were stronger as well.

Keep the main things the main things.

The ART of Delegation

3 Embrace

Ask Yourself these questions.

Are you willing to realize you must embrace your own challenges?
Are you willing to learn how to reward and recognize the achievements of others?

Embrace. This is going to be a big step.

To embrace means so many things. The first things have a lot to do with looking in the mirror. After all, the ART of Delegation starts with you being aware of what is stopping you from delegating, and embracing the fact that moving forward will include making mistakes; it will involve trusting people that are in your life; it will involve letting other people make mistakes and getting "things" back on track.

To Embrace: to accept or support (a belief, or theory) willingly and enthusiastically.

27

Let us talk about First Steps. You may have to embrace that…

- …you may need a new **communication style** and you may have to repair relationships that may have been affected by the "old" communication style.
- …you may have to **change the group** of people that you surround yourself with – take an inventory of their skills and how they can/could participate.
- … you may have to **improve your gratitude**, appreciation, and/or rewards habits. Thanking people often and appropriately is a key in the ART of delegation.

A little deeper on Embracing:

- Embrace your ideas and vision - that it is valuable and worthy. This takes unbridled confidence.
- Embrace that most times the first "swing" at things – a rough draft is not the best one. This takes determination and forethought.
- Embrace that you may be wrong
- Embrace that business ideas, and projects need flexibility and how you thought things were going to "go", may not take the path you first thought. This takes emotional maturity.

As you can tell, embracing is an important part of the process in order to really "get it".

Let us start the idea of a project. It really does not matter what type of project for this example.

Most of the time, people start a project because they are passionate about something. Agreed? They have a skill, talent or ability that is marketable, sellable, or usable.

Let us assume that a business, trade, hobby is started; and now has the potential of being "more" – more needs to be manufactured, or more needs to be serviced or simply just more of your time needs to be given.

If you are an aspiring entrepreneur, you have been to this spot. Frustration may set in, and the desire and fun of what the project once was, has now become drudgery.

Changing gears.

If everyone pitches in to the goal (the project, the company, the idea); the jobs get done, the vision is realized and the goals are achieved.

Embrace: it is mostly an introspection of what you are good at and what you are NOT good at.

- "What you love to do" vs "needs to be done"
- What is best done by others?
- What 'shouldn't' I do?

By processing just these three questions will get you closer to the ART of Delegation; in fact, it is why the book is subtitled "Do what you love to do".

Listen: Listen to others, their ideas, their vision

Ignore: Shut out distractions and create boundaries

Embrace: Accept and support your strengths and opportunities and those of your team (your family or co-workers)

These are all huge self-awareness steps. Your company, team and your family will see a difference in you once you truly commit to these few habits.

As an entrepreneur myself, I realized early on that the best part of a new business was the camaraderie; the times I could help partners, co-workers become more than what they ever thought they could be.

…the worst part is that I tried to do everything myself and things that I was able to do, but not very well, became a source of stress and discontentment.

The reason for this book. The reason for the training I do.

Embracing is a key component to many challenges we face in our lives. Business life, family life, social life. Relationships have more quality if we can all teach each other to be more self-aware and embrace the qualities that add value and those that do not add value.

Read that again….

Relationships, of all kinds, have more quality if we can all teach each other to be more self-aware and embrace the qualities that **add** value and those that **do not add** value to our jobs, to our families, to our lives.

30

The question is for you: What are your skills, talents, and abilities that you can share? What ideas do you have that can contribute to your workplace, your community, or the world?

What are some things that you must EMBRACE to make all your dreams come true?

Here is the ACTION ITEM part of the chapter.

- The one where you can choose some behaviors to practice to get you more efficient in EMBRACING which is a prework for DELEGATION.

- What do you enjoy doing? And in this case, I am not talking about a hobby or a family matter. In this case, what part of the processes really make you happy, and you are encouraged to do them

- What are the tasks and chores that you know "just enough about" that make you dangerous; but, that take an enormous amount of time to complete – and you may have to "do over" because they were not completed to a standard that serves the project.

- What activities or tasks are you an EXPERT in; and could teach another member of your team to adopt.

- What classes can you take to improve your performance at doing the projects you love.

My challenges:

- As my business grew, I needed to learn how to manage the projects that needed to be done faster, or on a larger scale.

- I could no longer do things that kept me from my goals.

- I had to learn how to hire the best, and not settle.

- My role was now being the cheerleader, teacher, or disciplinarian as projects progressed.
- Embrace change -staying focused on the outcome and not the details of how – allowing others to grow

- Embrace "time table" that setting realistic goals was important to the team's success

- Embrace my team's "pain points" – things that were disabling the project or process.

FACTS About EMBRACING

- Business and People Change, the more flexible you are to the HOWS (how things get completed) and remain focused on the outcome with milestones will create the best combination for success.

- Spend time in the planning process and share with

everyone who is on the team, of what your vision is.

- As a business owner or project manager, it is imperative to have check-ins with the team. Some call these "check-ins" milestones; but could also be considered a review of the progress while continuing to review those milestones as it relates to the goal completion.

A Quick Story:

Unfortunately, most people will never understand what "doing what you love to do, effortlessly" means.

When you embrace everything in life that comes your way as an opportunity, there is a magic to it. I am not exaggerating when I say that I wake up every day with an excitement to start the day. I do not need caffeine or supplements to "get me started" in the morning.

Embracing means that you allow new ideas, new adventures, or experiences to manifest. Dream big! Trust yourself that you can make things happen. I never ask HOW something will happen; I embrace the confidence that I know I can make anything happen.

I also embrace the true gifts I have around me. The people that I need to manifest dreams always show up. No matter what the challenge, talented people find their way into my life. This includes my foundation, the blessings of my family and friends.

For those not as fortunate with a solid foundation, that foundation will start with you. Embrace all that you are, and all that you can improve.

When it comes to delegation, people want to see that confidence. When you embrace all that there is there is no obstacle that cannot be overcome.

4 EMPOWER

Ask Yourself these questions.

Who could you mentor?
Do you continually challenge your team?
How do you grow your teams?

This may be my favorite part of the book. To empower people is the most emotional thing I have ever experienced, especially when those people succeed as a result of their efforts.

Empowerment may be the most challenging habit for a person that has not embraced the qualities needed to empower people.

To Empower someone means to give them the means to achieve something to become stronger or more successful. For someone to be empowered they must be delegated to effectively and have full support.

I think about the best experiences that I had being empowered and the times that I feel like I empowered people.

A simple example comes to mind.

What does empowerment look like?

- Think about your child learning to walk
- Think about a graduation from anything
- Think about an award

Encouraging, empowering TALK is important. Encouraging, empowering LISTENING is crucial. Encouraging, empowering ACTIONS and rewards is EPIC

Another question is what happens if you have a person on your team that has the skills, but not the training? Has the smarts but not the "degree"? Has the desire but not the skills?

To empower means to give someone the MEANS to be able to achieve things. What does that mean?

- School / Classes
- Provide an opportunity to learn from others
- On the job training
- Encouraging practice

How many ways can you think of how you have been encouraged and were trusted to TRY.

The goal of empowerment is to provide information and permission for the team to address problems and achieve goals.

If people have what they need to solve their own problems, it frees up YOUR time to challenge yourself in other areas.

There are key factors to empowerment:

- Build Trust
- Solicit Feedback
- Offer Instruction or Direction
- Provide Discovery Options
- Show Appreciation
- Understand Limits

Building Trust

Trust needs to be an understanding between two people. It also means that you are responsible for mistakes that are made by others. Trust is the most important factor in the ART of Delegation. Trust means that all things are truthful in the relationship. Trust also means that both parties are emotionally intelligent enough to share feedback and provide honest feedback about capabilities of the individual or the team.

Solicit Feedback

Feedback is important in the ART of Delegation. Milestone checkpoints have also been used as a form of feedback – how the project is going and what the expectations are of completion.

Offer Instruction or Direction

I used to say "I may not know the answer, but I know how to get it." Instruction and guidance is imperative, even if you are not the provider of the instruction or guidance.

Provide Discovery Options

One of the best things I did was write instructions on how to do everything in my companies. The instructions were updated with new ideas and improvements at each milestone. Making instructions/manuals with 'how to' do everything relieves the manager from instructional duties and empowers the person to find their own answers.

Show Appreciation

There are many ways to show appreciation. Simple "thank you" 's go a long way, others prefer public recognition, certificates, trophies, days off with pay or a coffee coupon. However, it is a crucial part of the ART of Delegation, and missing this habit can be destructive to the team.

Understand Limits

What we think can happen, what we hope can happen is another self-awareness habit which is important for you and your team. When successful people are on a goal mission, sometimes the desire to get the job done prevents them from setting limits. Quality control limits, timing limits, training limits, physical limits. The ART of Delegation requires a sense of what can be done, and how many people or tools are needed to complete a task.

Who have you empowered? What feelings did you get from the empowerment? What miraculous things have happened to you and your businesses because you empowered someone?

In my case: As a result of being empowered and empowering others.

- I am who I am because I was empowered
- Businesses flourished
- Changed family dynamics
- Inspired change with other people and businesses

By reading this book, even up to this chapter, you can see where empowering people can also empower you.   This is the time again to take some personal inventory into mastering the ART of Delegation.

How are your
- Listening skills
- How are you shutting out distractions
- How are Embracing what needs to be changed in order to effectively delegate to your teams
- What are your favorite Empowerment stories, and how have you empowered others?

Action items to work on this very valuable skill of Empowering.

- First, if you struggle with retention or hiring the best, that would be the first action item to review. Empowering people means a huge investment of time; spending that valuable time on an invaluable teammate is crushing – in many ways. The action item here could be simply learning how to interview people better for the project, job or activity you are requiring them to do.

- ASK QUESTIONS!! Ask more questions than anything! Ask for commitment to time tables and activities. Utilize the teammates' answers to formulate milestones.

- Reward, reward, reward. Here is the tricky part. How do you reward and empower behavior? Some folks will enjoy money, others may enjoy time off, gift cards, or a group luncheon.

- Put in your calendar daily to reward, or compliment, serve or empower someone daily – this activity can be related to a project, a team, a new business or your household. Once you see the power behind empowering another human being, it will be something you will never want to stop.

FACTS ABOUT EMPOWERING People

- There is a balance to make people feel empowered around you. Too much, or too little guidance throws off the balance – ask questions – a simple "do you have everything you need to accomplish the goal?" is an easy and effective question

- In delegation: there is one leader, one person who is guiding the ship. When you empower people, you leave room for other leaders to grow. Both have their place in projects, learning how to delegate will eventually help you learn how to empower your team more effectively. (I make people "captains" and "lieutenants" of specific parts of the team – I delegate to those captains, and allow them to get empowered and guide their team to success- or have them "report on their successes" at the team meeting)

- Allow people to make an impact. Make sure to publicly recognize that impact!

- Promote future opportunities as a result of empowering actions. When people are empowered, they tend to increase their skill sets as well. Remember that empowerment is about guidance and allowing the team to self-correct, adjust and identify the "pain points" of the project.

A Quick Story:

Empowering is something many people get to experience naturally, but many do not know how to perform the task. It is a learned behavior and somewhat of a privilege to be able to do.

"Empower" others. What does it mean? For me, it

meant encouraging others to do something that is for the betterment of themselves by making them stronger and more confident.

When you empower people, you are helping someone do what they might not be able to do on their own, you are giving them the power to perform and hopefully succeed.
Empowering someone can be as simple as sending someone positive vibes in a text message, a hand written letter or just a quick call telling people you were thinking of them and seeing how they are doing.

I remember in my early 20's I discovered what it meant to Empower people. I encouraged a few friends to take a leap of faith in my business idea. It required them to have faith in me and faith in themselves.

My first company was a mall-based kiosk business that offered cell phone repair and fashionable accessories back in the late 90's. I empowered my friends to quit their jobs and become entrepreneurs. The company was very successful and it changed the trajectory of my, and many others' lives.

You can change the trajectory of your life any time you want. When you change the trajectory of others' lives for the better, you are creating legacy. Through the ART of Delegation Legacies will be made!

5 PERSONAL TIME

Ask Yourself these questions.

**When was the last time you took time off?
How do you create quality personal time?
Are you uncomfortable with alone time?**

This seems like it would be the fun part of the book – and YES it will be! But there is an elephant in the room that needs to be discussed first.

When you experience and get "used to" going 100 miles an hour; when you always have competing priorities; when you are constantly trying to juggle an intense schedule. You may find it hard to let go of the grind or the constant need for drive.

Ironically, this is the FUN chapter; it is also one of the most challenging chapters. Entrepreneurs, driven people have a hard time slowing down and realizing that Personal time is truly the "secret sauce" to a great life.

I called Personal Time the reward. In some cases, it is a curse. Let us break personal time down into two parts.

The first category is YOUR personal time. Time to recharge, renew and refresh – work on your health, your relationships, your adventure time, or your quiet time.

The second category would be considered personal time that would be revolutionary for your business; time to learn new skills (like delegation), to learn new concepts, or ways to improve your business acumen.

Let us just start with the business part of Personal Time. What do you do to stay fresh in your industry?

Some ideas of how to stay on top of your industry while enjoying personal time.

- I read / listen to podcasts
- I visit and experience competition – truly experience
- I engage with other professionals – network
- I listen more than ever
- I read reviews, not all good reviews: in fact, the bad reviews are the best teachers

Does this still sound like work?
- Change your approach.
- Change the idea in your head and enjoy other professionals in your industry.
- Keep any jealousy or critique at bay, so you can

46

enjoy the fruits of someone else's labor

One quick thing I forgot to mention. When you are not used to having personal time, it may become an emotional experience. Meaning, you may **not** LIKE **not** being busy.

I remember the first time I had successfully delegated a project. I found myself with "time on my hands." Instead of doing any of the productive activities (reading, visiting, experiencing) I turned into a micro manager – which now I realized was an emotional response to the mis-managed time. (this is a killer for empowering people)

My team said things like "don't you have something else to do?" "Why don't you go to lunch" or worse, setting up time for me to be "out of the office".

I was lucky.

Other teams may do things like "fall apart" or "resent" the leader or the project. You may have been a part of a team that suffered or, worse, ended like that.

So here it is! Somewhat of the "secret sauce" to managing, delegating, leading, overseeing... YOUR PERSONAL TIME.

With regards to work or career, personal time is crucial. What do you do to decompress from your day? I do not practice all these rituals but I have routines that work:

The car has become my sanctuary

- I listen to podcasts or books
- I listen to my favorite "charge me up" music
- I have ALONE time every day to "process"
- I eat alone once a day to collect all the thoughts in my head
- I journal (voice to text if in the car)

Think about some of the things mentioned already in this book. Delegation involves trust and understanding of projects; a good leader who listens and can decipher when the milestones of projects are not getting met.

Being the best ME I could be made me better at delegating. I was able to see more opportunities in the team that was around me. I learned new things that we were able to challenge each other with. My understanding of my industry in the "big picture" allowed me to create greater opportunities.

Let us switch gears for a second and talk about REAL PERSONAL Time.

We all have choices every day in what we feed our minds, souls, and bodies. This personal time section is how you feed yourself. Do what you LOVE to do! Spend time on yourself in knowing what nutrition is best for you, what activities you love to do, what places you like to visit – you get the point.

Love Yourself first and foremost and do the things that keep you healthy.

I told myself I wanted better for me. No one is perfect,

48

and certainly everyone has an opinion or a judgment to share.

- I love to travel.
- I get overwhelmed at seeing beautiful countryside.
- I made a conscious decision watch what I ate, and stayed active
- I stay away from toxic TV, people, and mindless conversations.

Here was the magic for me. In my personal time **I FOCUS**.

I learned from a lot of people; **whatever you focus on grows**. If I focused on negativity, negativity grew. When I focused on solutions, the opportunity was abundant.

My challenge was to make my personal time the best that it could be - to allow me to grow my amazing family; to share my insights and successes with my children; to keep my vows to my beautiful wife; and to be a contribution to my community.

When you focus on the "things" that matter, business, and success come easier. Laws of Attraction will support this, every religion has this simple focus on you as a foundation; and you will find that every facet of your life becomes manageable.

Amazingly enough, people will feel comfortable delegating to you; as well as a better relationship to delegate to others.

Some ACTION items for this chapter; actually, relatively easy to do.

Schedule "me" time; whatever that means for you. Lunch alone, drives on your favorite scenic road, libraries, meditation, yoga, time with family and do not let anything interrupt it.

I had franchise owners that were hugely successful, mildly successful and others who were, honestly, complete failures. What was the big difference? The crash-and-burners were the 100 hour a week people; they always were frantic, arguably always in a bad mood (from lack of sleep and poor food choices) and never took time off.

The successful group (either highly or mildly) delegated. They hired people. They took time off. Their hours of operation were not 24/7. They created a success footprint people could follow.

In this chapter, get a grasp on perception. If you get comments from your family and friends like, "I'm worried you are going to burn out" or "you're always working, and we hardly have time to spend together", "when do you sleep?" **Those are tell-tales.**

When was the last time you spent time with a close friend, or your spouse, or your children. QUALITY TIME… not interrupted by technology or others? If you cannot remember, then RIGHT NOW…put that date in your calendar, and hit the word "repeat."

- Practice your listening skills
- Tell people you love and care for them and give examples of how important they are in your life
- Embrace how much you are loved, liked, respected
- Experience something new with a friend, love, family member and make a memory

I heard this quote once – probably one of my work peers – "have you ever been so busy that you forget to put gas in the car?" ... The fuel metaphor is obviously equivalent to your personal time to recharge, refresh and renew.

.... Ready for a mid-book check in!?....

Before we move on. I want to review what we have touched on in these chapters.

Most of what we strive for in our lives; whether it be with a business venture, better relationships, more time to enjoy life can be achieved if we just focus on what is important. Most of what we need to focus on is "inside work" meaning that it is most important to self-reflect and find the things we can improve within ourselves; rather than "trying to change the world".

The ART of Delegation and the steps I have outlined so far will ultimately be felt by you; but seen by so many other people. Truly, what brings on stress; and/or stressful situations has everything to do with our reactions to things; our abilities to complete tasks; our abilities to get "things" done in a timely manner.

I put together the ACTION ITEMS at the end of each chapter with the intention of having you, the reader, experience the difference in some of the skill sets you have now, and improving them.

By improving skills like LISTENING and IGNORING you are showing by your actions how to actively engage and build trust with people.

By improving the ways, you EMBRACE and EMPOWER your skills, talents, and abilities; you show others your confidence in yourself and the confidence you have in them and their abilities.

By improving how you use your PERSONAL TIME to recharge and refocus; it shows your "audience" that success is sweeter when you have a balance.

Think about it. Have you seen the business owner that is always stressed out, working ALL the time, and MAKING the business themselves, seemingly without help - with the sacrifice being the personal time, health, and mental wellness? Who is writing books about how to be more of THAT?

With the steps I have outlined in the book, the goal is to help you learn how to delegate; but it is truly the ART of Delegation; so that you, the reader, can find ways to do ALL the "elements" of what you LOVE to do, and not what you feel like you "HAVE" to do.   I think the new saying is "I GET" to do those things that I love and not get mixed up in the turmoil of things that HAVE to be done.

When you allow people to become part of the process of a new business, a new venture, a non-profit, a for profit, a project or anything else that would speak success to you - you change lives.

That is right! I said it! By Learning the ART of Delegation, you will change others' lives as it changes your success quotient. In other words, while you are becoming wildly successful, so are others.

Why do I keep CAPITALIZING ART in the ART of Delegation?

It stands for **ATTITUDE, RESPONSIBILITY** and **TRUST** - technically the title **ART of Delegation" Do what you Love to do**; to delegate effectively and efficiently - you must have the ART component.

In all these chapters, the underlying outcome will be a better management style, better **ART** for all components of your life. By the way - in finance, **ART** means **Annual Renewable Term**; every year, read this book again!

A Quick Story:

I have always been one of those guys that gets energy from people. I like to be busy and around people because it makes me feel wanted, important and I besides I am one of those people that likes to chat.

I found a balance of being "in the scene" with and without people that has allowed me the ability to express myself while having the personal time I need to process things.

In the first chapter of my life (high school through first business ventures), I lived for others, doing what others did, I tried to fit in, I followed the heard as some people refer to it as. I also had a family.

It did not matter how hectic my day was, I would always say yes to anything and stack the day with as much as I could to constantly stay super busy. (sound familiar?)

As long as I could sit down for 45 minutes to have a meal at the end of the day (often with my notepad or laptop engaged) , by myself to just take time to reflect on the day and gather my thoughts, I was happy.

My life was a grind Monday – Thursdays with that perpetual Wheel of Purpose. I tried to make sure my personal time Friday through Sunday was not interrupted. So I worked what seemed like 24 hours day Monday through Thursday.

I felt like it was a time when I needed to "run solo" so I could "pave the road" without any interruptions. A typical entrepreneur feeling of wanting be faster, more, cutting edge at the risk of sleep.

Part of my work weeks, I spent time driving my RV to locations. I recall on several occasions my wife saying, "Why don't you go take a road trip"!

Even though I was already on the road, my ears would perk up like a dog that was just tossed a milk bone! Immediately I would look on the map for a destination and my "work drive" would turn into something else.

There is something about getting behind the wheel of my RV that just put me in almost a trance. A state of Freedom to where all my thoughts and worries would fall into place. Long drives to me with my favorite music are like others' spa experiences or the cabana on the Riveria.

The point is whatever you consider personal time just make sure you do it. Personal time is whatever puts your mind as ease to collect your thoughts.

I hope you are enjoying this so far…

…on to some GUT work!

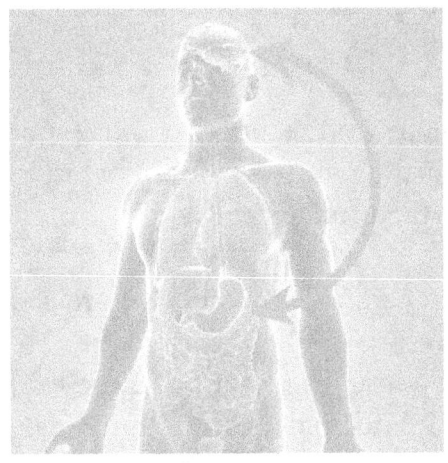

6 TRUST YOUR GUT

Ask Yourself these questions.

What physical thing happens when you get stressed?
Have you identified any past experiences that may be affecting your decision making?

Where the heck is your "GUT" Anyway?

I know where mine is, it is right around my Adam's apple in my throat and it burns or some similar sensation when I'm feeling not safe, or I think someone is lying, or I feel like I am not getting into something I shouldn't.

In the spirit of delegation my gut gets a workout! However, there is a healthy reason for this chapter.

- First, identify where your gut is.

57

- What are the symptoms or scenarios you think your gut is active

This gut/brain connection is a real thing! There is a linking between the emotional and cognitive centers of the brain with intestinal function.

It is why we cannot eat when we are sad or hurt; I am sure you have heard of the "divorce diet" – which I thank God that I know nothing about. I have experienced a sick feeling when I anticipated something happening to my children on the playground or jumping on furniture.

Why are we talking about GUTS? Because people say things like "Trust your gut" in business; in relationships, so if people are going to use the GUT as a GPS, we should at least know something about it and how it plays a role in delegation.

How do you know to trust your gut?

I suppose it is like anything else. Trial and Error. I was born with my gut feeling and it matured over my lifetime into this "trigger" when I thought something was wrong or when I thought I should "Just do it." I have the same gut feeling about people sometimes - good and bad.

Have you ever had a gut feeling that was wrong? Ever misjudged a person for their abilities? Ever totally trusted someone that broke your confidence?

The gut brain connection is oddly a learned behavior.

58

You can change your reaction to that "gut" feeling by challenging your gut feeling with questions like:

- What did that person do, that is giving me the odd feeling?
- Am I having this feeling because I am triggered or is the circumstance or person reminding me of something?

Can you think of a time when you could challenge your gut feeling because you were wrong?

- Misjudged a person or their abilities
- Thought you were going to have a terrible time, and you had one of the best times?
- Thought you did better than you did?
- Realized that you were projecting an expected outcome; and were sabotaging it?

Here is the challenge with Trusting your gut.

- If you have a lot of experience, your gut is probably pretty 'tuned;'
- If you do not have a lot of experience or trauma in your life, you may be more susceptible to mistakes.
- If you struggle with boundaries, you may have trouble trusting your gut
- Do you 'second guess' yourself?

Entrepreneurs have been "stereotyped" to have no gut feelings. I do not necessarily agree. In fact, I have even heard entrepreneurship is like jumping out of a plane and figuring it out on the way down. They have a gut feeling that despite a "rocky ride" they will be successful. .

The key to this story is the entrepreneur still jumps out of the proverbial plane. Making mistakes along the way is expected. Failures are expected.

Trusting your gut is what keeps people safe. Not everyone is not an entrepreneur or has that intestinal fortitude to take a chance on themselves.

Trusting your gut can also prevent mistakes; allow you to see abilities and inabilities in people based on how they make you feel; and keep people from achieving their highest self.

This GUT thing is tricky....

Let us say that you trust your GUT:

- You trust yourself
- You trust people are telling you the truth
- You trust that past performance will predict future outcomes

Be smart about your choices. And ask yourself these questions when your gut is "acting up":

- Why am I feeling this way?
- What are the consequences to not trusting my gut?
- Am I scared? Or is there a reason for my feeling?
- What will I miss out on?

I think back to every decision I made in business. I felt confident, but there was always the emotion of questioning whether I was doing the right thing.

The answers were always yes, I did do the right thing. Looking back, I can see where I could have done things differently, but the outcomes were just as brilliant. My GUT guided me. I'm sure there were times it guided me out of things too.

The message here is TRUST YOUR GUT. If you do not feel like you can trust your gut... then spend some PERSONAL TIME and figure it out.

Things to consider, practice, identify and embrace - Our ACTION ITEM section, if you will.

Gut reactions
- Could be something wrong in your body
- A relationship that does not "feel" right
- A Career choice that makes you uneasy
- A Move (could be house or business) that does not feel right
- Potential Danger
- Help someone in need

You can call gut reactions "intuition", and sometimes those feelings are related to a past experience you have had. Other times it may be "nerves" for trying something new.

Either way, **trust your intuition; trust your gut.**

It should not be judged or dismissed, and no two intuitions are the same. If you feel like something is not right; trust your feelings and take action to remedy it. Do not let others convince you or bully you into making decisions.

Ways to deepen your trust in your GUT:

- Meditate - start and end your day with peace
- Be mindful of your decisions and the "mood" you are in when you make them. (like mindful eating, for instance)
- Breathing exercises and stretching throughout the day, rather than that caffeine or sugar boost in the afternoon. Paying attention to what your body needs
- Try new things - could be an outfit or a new hobby
- Pay attention to unexpected surprises and happy occurrences that seem to happen by chance. Trust and believe that however you "think" that occurrence happened - make note of it. Take an inventory or at very least log the event!
- Journaling is another great way to remind yourself of feelings and occurrences that are worthy of noting
- Daydream. Dream Big. Allow yourself to have those joyful moments and "castles in the sky" without judgment.

I want to repeat one more portion of these last few sentences. Do not let others "persuading" abilities convince you or bully you into making decisions. The world has become one of this "cancel culture" and many "ill-will's" if you are not a conformist.

By allowing others to sway you, think what that looks like from the viewpoint of those watching you and about to get their direction from you.

Stand firm in your convictions; make every decision with the best intentions; and play out what the outcomes may be. Not every decision will be right, however, the decisions with the best intentions will be honorable, trustworthy, and correctable.

How is trusting your gut going to help you with the ART of Delegation? **Delegation is best served with trust**; if you cannot trust yourself, others will have a tough time trusting you.

A Quick Story:

This is my favorite Super Power of all the skills I have ever learned. Like Kenny Rogers lyrics in the Gambler, "know when to hold 'em, know when to fold 'em, when to walk away and when to run.

Trusting your gut is using your intuition to make imperative decisions that could dramatically impact your life and well-being. It is a known fact that the lack of decision-making causes stress, and of course, we all know what stress does. Do not stay in "limboland", sometimes a bad decision is better than no decision – and "moving on" will lead you to a much more peaceful life.

Have you ever heard the expression "A bad decision is better than no decision"? It has held true in my life for sure.

Trusting yourself is a key component in trusting your gut. Being "in tune" to your "gut reactions" can help advance yourself in to a realm of possibilities and adventures. Opportunities do not always necessarily feel right or easy at the time – timing is important.

I always tell people "If it doesn't make you pucker, it may not be right for you"; in other words, if you are looking at something like a business or a relationship and you don't get a little anxious; excited; passionate; burn a little, it may not be worth the risk.

.   Sometimes opportunities are presented to us because they are answers to problems, or identify things we do not want to do. Trusting your gut should keep you in your lane and on purpose.

In the 90s, I had a great business idea. (I talked about it in the last chapter). After pitching the idea to a friend and to my dad, neither of which went as expected. "Sounds like a great idea", my dad said, "don't you have a credit card?" I was confused. He couldn't be asking me to put this $3500 risk on a credit card. "Go to the credit union and tell the teller you want a "cash advance", don't look at the interest rate, just get the money to start your business"

Because of that advice I was able to save $1000 and got the $2500 I needed. I was a bartender and very nervous about maxing out my credit card. However, I had confidence in myself and my abilities. Were there bumps in the road? YES. Within 4 years, I turned that $2500 into several million dollars because I trusted my gut, I listened and I embraced all the experiences.

There is no such thing as failure. That statement defines my life; and I'm so proud of all the people who believe in me and continue to make success stories like this in their lives.

100% of the pitches you do not swing at, will never become home runs.

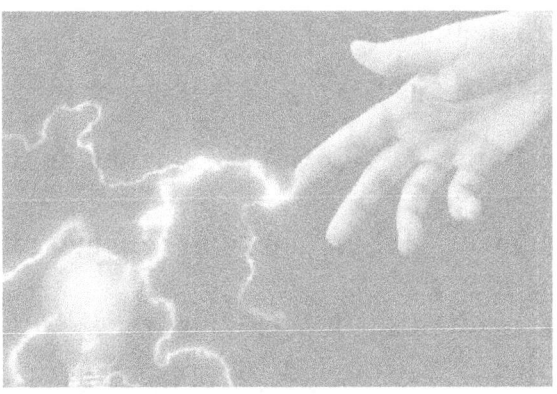

7 ENERGIZE

Ask Yourself these questions.

Where do you get your energy from?
How do you exude energy?
How do you manage others' energy?

There are so many ways to describe Energy in business. How to energize a business? How to energize ourselves in business? How does Energy affect the ART of Delegation?

As we discussed ART in the ART of Delegation- Attitude, Responsibility and Trust. Energy is an attitude. It is a feeling. It is a source of fuel. It is a driving force.

First, reviewing these chapters, this is the part where Personal Time is so important. You must be able to provide energy to your projects; energy to the team; energy to the activities in order to create the best environment for success.

I have figured out "things" that stole my energy and how I remedied them/removed them/ fixed them; I hope

67

identifying these things will help you in creating a great work, home, or team environment.

Failures happen. My reaction to failures was a huge downer for my team and those around me. My favorite quote by Thomas Edison: "The most certain way to succeed is to try one more time".

Funny, I never treated my children the way I treated my business failures. What could I change? I started using the same philosophy with my co-workers as I did with my children's sports teams and the activities, they were in. When they missed the ball, or fell; I yelled "get up! Go, Go, Go! Try again" ... At work; I started doing the same with my team (with **not much** less enthusiasm).

Long term planning. I would focus and create my long-term plan but would not share it with my team. No reason, really. I just figured that they had their tasks at hand, and they did not need to know what my thoughts were for the future.

Once I realized what knowing the long-term plan meant to the team; I understood how **not** telling them sucked the energy out of the team.

The team was much more interested in the future, in their future, in how they could contribute more once I shared my vision than I had realized.

I tried it: I shared an overview of where I envisioned the success of one of the companies. The months after the "announcement"; employees were going back to school, getting certifications to improve their skills; and they were

68

communicating with each other in different ways.

When people (the whole team) are included in the vision, those that see themselves as part of the long term plan change their trajectory (Improved their skills, achieved other credentials to compliment the vision).

When people see themselves as just as much a part of the long-term plan as the plan itself; magic happens.

Make tough decisions; do not delay. I have learned this lesson the hard way - many times. When to say "enough is enough" with a venture, an employee, or a company.

I have referred to it many times throughout the book, you are being watched and identified as a leader. The decisions you make, and how quickly you make them will be discussed with your team, with or without you present.

The easiest "tough decision" a leader must make is terminating a relationship with an employee that is not serving their purpose. Your ability to be able to identify and correct the 'weak link' on a team is crucial to the energy "thermometer."

In a few words, just understand that the "challenged" employee will take up more of your time; take away from the energy you should be giving to your top employee.

You can replace the word "employee" with project, business, venture, by the way.

When you make the tough decisions quickly, you

allow people to resume good work; you allow new life to be instilled in the venture/company etc.

I remember one of those "lifelong sayings" - People don't leave companies or ventures, they leave bad managers. I firmly believe that great managers are ones who learn the ART of Delegation.

There are many ways that this ENERGIZING chapter can go. Of course, what I have described so far is the Energy around your company, your employees, and your vision.

What about YOUR Energy. "The boss's energy". How you walk and convey confidence, energy, and passion. With the challenges that we all face of authenticity, cancel culture, news, politics (local and national) our energy can take a beating.

Are you sleeping well? Are you eating well? What is your demeanor when you enter the office? What is your energy level at networking events? At family parties?

The ART of Delegation is a full body activity. Whether or not you will be successful in delegation is a "whole vibe", the new hip way to say who you are! It's what you think, how you act, how you carry yourself, how others perceive you, your vocabulary, diction, your tone, your body language and the way you make decisions.

… one more discussion about Energy in the world….

Energy can be felt, conveyed, watched, and practiced.

70

There is, in nature, an **energy pyramid**.

The Energy Pyramid is made up of Producers (bottom rung), Consumers (middle rungs) and Decomposers (top rung).

As with all things in nature, living things have a natural life progression. My relation to this energy pyramid, for myself, is identifying the producers, the consumers, and the decomposers in every situation.

Nature has a way of explaining things simplistically; and most times the concepts are completely relatable and congruent to business. We have decisions to make as to how to utilize, manage and dispose or recycle energy.

Let us look a little deeper into this Energy Pyramid

We all need energy **producers**; great idea makers, the creators, the song writers, the trend setters, the inventors, and the business minds that find the "missing" things that we need.

The producers will tend to give you the best NEW ideas, or additions to make your idea even better! They also could need to be managed - their tendencies are explosions of energy - fast talkers and fast movers. Think of how much energy a budding plant needs to break through the soil.

This group may not be the best at communication. They may be hard to tolerate in the office or at home, but managed effectively the producers will soar with the proper guidance and delegation.

71

An example: Energy producers are typically "people: that add value in whatever they touch. Energy producers can be **activities** that add value, like team building exercises, yoga, or a good book; or people that invent a breakthrough product.

An example at home: I was aware of intelligent children, including my own, that tended to get bored; or worse, get in trouble when their energy wasn't managed effectively at school.

Give energy producers "too much time on their hands" and they are the least effective.

Word to the wise, if your child comes home **day after day** with "no homework" because they did it already... get them involved in something extra-curricular. At work, these are described as "stretch assignments."

The **consumers** are needed to utilize the energy and manage it to its best function - with the hope that they will continue to influence the other consumers to manage and utilize its' worth.

The **consumers** are the general population that also need to be managed. If by now, they have ultimate trust in you, the consumers will be the most visible energy on your team and in your life and the most eager.

Often, the **consumers** will run with whatever you ask them to do, mostly without question. Much of this energy is emotional energy.

An example: Think of a plant or a tree as an energy consumer. They take the energy of the sun, soil and food sources grow strong; sometimes they bear fruit; sometimes they become breathtakingly beautiful.

Relating this concept to a person, this could be your consumer base of your product; or a team mate that is the company's best billboard; or the employee that feeds off others energy to build their own energy force (ripple effect)

The **decomposers at home and work** will hopefully reuse the discarded energy to recycle and put back into "nature" the tools to regenerate more energy.

An example: when I first heard these concepts, I said, "oh I get it, the decomposers are the people that squash all the bad ideas; or take the energy away from things that take away from the overall vision."

After understanding the concept a little better, decomposition means the breakdowns of all the good and bad; the no longer usable, to be recycled. This process is used on a cellular level and in every other "hierarchy," cells, plants, animals, and humans.

I know this may be funny to some, but I relate my auditing team, my accountants, my money people as the **decomposers** in my world.

My team reports to me what is good and what is bad; what I should spend my energy on, and what is a losing battle. For all intents and purposes, they are my gatekeepers to my recycle bin.

The decomposers will give you the raw data, of what to keep and what to dispose of; mostly very clear about YES or NO answers and very logical without emotion to keep you focused on your goals.

ACTION ITEMS

- Identify any challenges you may have with your energy. Are you the best you that you can be every day with your "people"?
- How can you reward and recognize the energy Producers, Consumers and Decomposers in your workplace; at home and on your teams. What purposes do they serve and what guidance do they need?
- How do you visibly deal with failures?
- Are you sharing your long-term plans with the people that can help you make those goals a reality?
- What decisions have you been putting off? What are you "dealing" with that you need to remove so your energy is better spent elsewhere?

My Challenges:
- I love a good challenge, and sometimes have a hard time walking away from something just because it is a challenge. Make sure you have regular check in's with your team to decide whether energy is being utilized in the best way.
- I try to maintain good energy through my diet, exercise, vacations, and personal time – my challenge

is to keep it up good routines all the time, so I do not experience the "low" energy feeling.

FACTS ABOUT ENERGY in BUSINESS: Or ways you maintain energy in the workplace:

- Organization and Priorities are Paramount
- Pay attention to the décor and colors in your space
- Focus on outcomes and allow people to grow!
- Put people in the right positions so that they enjoy the work they are doing.
- Make tough decisions to enable people to do their best work

If you see challenges with the energy in your business, or around projects; please refer to the **Trust Your Gut** chapter and find out why your energy may be low. Remember if you as the leader have doubts, your employees will "smell" it on you.

In the ART of Delegation; Attitude, Responsibility and Trust are the keys to having good energy; in the workplace and around the projects at hand.

A Quick Story:

I mentioned earlier I get energy from people. I am constantly being told by my peers and family that I always radiate a lot of positive energy. But where does it come from?

Is it something I was born with, is it a god given talent?

High energy people can sometimes me a turnoff as well. Here is where I struggle.

My good friend and life coach says "John, you must remember you are a QuickStart. You come into the room sometimes with lots of energy, but you can also be perceived as a Bull in a China shop. Just barreling through and not paying attention to what is happening around you" That is not true, nor my intention, however perception becomes reality.

I watch how my energy is perceived by others. I try to maintain the perfect energy for me and for my team. We all fall short of the energy bus sometimes, that is when surrounding yourself with the right energy can pull you through!

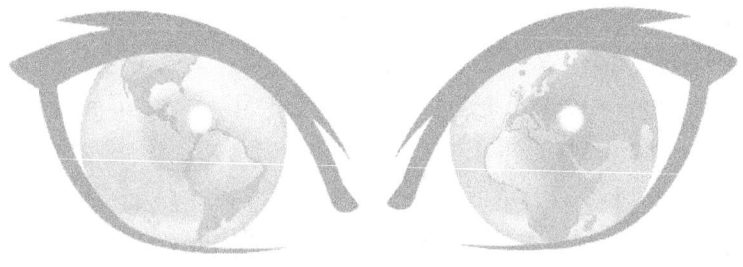

8 VISION & PLAN

Ask Yourself these questions.

What is your planning process?
Who is included in the planning once you have a
vision for a new project, business, or venture?

Let us discuss the definition of Vision Planning. When I first heard this, I thought it was two different things. Vision, having the idea; and planning, meaning execution of that idea.

Who knew, the concept of Vision Planning is a great tool; especially in the ART of Delegation. There is a process of how this works. First, the definition:

"Vision planning is an ongoing process that requires **complete workforce engagement**. Your staff helps to provide insight into potential issues or challenges as well as opportunities in the process of forming the plan, and having their input considered solidifies their commitment to successfully carrying out the plan" (Indeed.com)

Essentially, the vision could be the foundation of your company, a new start up, or a project, or venture – and the planning is done as a group. Once again, a great concept to help with the ART of Delegation.

The CEO, You or Me, is held accountable for the Attitude, Responsibility, and the Trust – and the Delegation should be easy.

As the leader, you will need to make sure that you will have an effective Vision Plan framework:

- Two-way communication between individuals; a place to keep that communication

- Someone needs to prioritize concepts (You) – schedule meetings for this.

- Creativity and Innovation (may require interviewing or getting a new team member for innovations outside your team's abilities)

- A Culture for change, diversity, and growth

The way I see it, there are two ways to vision plan. You can plan with goals – writing goals, this is what we want to do, how we do it and why we do it.

I prefer more of an outcome-based vision planning. We set the vision together as a team, and then the team decides how to make it all happen – so, in all fairness you release the HOW it gets done.

When the HOW is formulated by the team and they have an opportunity to ebb and flow, especially in some of the ever-changing markets that we are in now – no one gets stuck on the HOW things get done.

My success with this has always been to make "captains" of areas that I knew we needed. For each team, there are sub or micro teams that can utilize each other as resources for the final "product"/goal/ vision to come to fruition.

Let us say, for instance, that you are opening up a company. In all company structures there are mainly areas – or Levers, is what I like to call them.

The HR Lever –The HR Lever is responsible for the foundation of which all things will rely on for structure and clarity.

The Operations Lever – this group is responsible for location, what equipment will be needed for the new company, intake, and maintenance of the machinery.

The Marketing Lever – this group is responsible for the brand and how that is broadcasted into the community you are providing your service or brand for.

The Sales Lever – this group is responsible for identifying how the company makes a profit. Sometimes

79

the group is also responsible for finding ways to decrease expenses.

As the CEO of the company, your responsibility is to shed light on the questions each group will ask you. The idea of an outcome-based vision plan is for the CEO to ask as many questions as they can to guide the team into success.

ASK MORE QUESTIONS? Yes!!

Let us examine just the HR Levers responsibility. What type of employees are you looking for? What skill set should they have?

The Operations Lever is about the daily "running" of the company. How much payroll do we need? What roles are required to accomplish our goals? What equipment do we need?

The Marketing lever is all about advertising and maintaining relationships. What should that look like?

Finally, the Sales lever, simply put is about sales. Putting dollars on the bottom line. Whenever I am planning for a business, the first thing I do is work on this part.

When you dissect the business vision planning like this, as an outcome, it gets clearer for everyone on the team what their roles are and what the deadlines are to complete them. It also helps when the business is up and running, when things are challenging to identify a team or teams that need to "go back to the drawing board and fix what is broken".

As the CEO, this allows you to rely on your teams and delegate effectively for long term success. Why can most CEOs have multiple companies? Because they build teams within the company to grow and succeed, so they can build more and more success.

ACTION ITEMS

- When you are ready to plan, make sure you include your team captains
- Build a process for visioning and planning, so everyone knows it is an event
- Make big decisions quick – like if a team is not completing their missions or goals.
- Are you sharing your long-term plans with the people that can help you make those goals a reality?

FACTS ABOUT VISION AND PLANNING: It is vital to have scheduled time to discuss this at each milestone in your company, venture, or relationship.

- Define what success looks like
- Monitor the successes and failures. Celebrate success and utilize the failures as a learning tool.
- Making everyone a part of the team is a vital part of the future of the company, the tenure of the employees and the FUN!

A Quick Story:

A Dream is a plan without execution. I have never been a Dreamer, even though I have always wanted to be. Or maybe simply, I do not define what I do as dream.

I have had successes and my fair share of failures as well. Failure to plan is often a byproduct of planning to fail, right?

My interpretation of vision or a visionary is that you see things that are not obvious. Your mind is envisioning things completed before they are even started. It is a God given talent. I believe that has been one of my strongest attributes, but like I mentioned earlier it comes with its problems.

I have embraced that I do not work well alone. I can plan and see things in solidarity but I need people around me to execute. I have been able to "swing the bat" so many times and hit singles, doubles and even home runs. The people that have been with me along my journey have helped me tremendously.

This is a good time to mention a few very influential people in my life: My Wife Laura, and my parents, Chris, Bryant, Blair, James, Luis, my brother David, Art, Dan, Paul 1 & 2, & Andy- Thank you!

Like any good leader or visionary, the positive supporting peers that you have in your life can make all the difference in achieving success. These people have helped me execute my visions, giving me pushback, sometimes just by being a sounding board. And for that I am ever grateful.

For the final step, you just must Believe!

9 BELIEVE

Ask Yourself these questions.

What Do you believe in?
Who Do you believe in?
What makes you "keep the faith"?

Believing in something is one of the most important factors in getting through life... in everything. When it comes to business, believing in yourself and believing in processes is vital. In this chapter, we are going to talk about belief systems.

First, I want to say that I was born and raised in the Catholic religion. My family used our connection to our Parish to create our family values and traditions. In the United States, to be an Italian Catholic family was not "rare," in fact, most of the neighborhoods were, for lack of a better word, "specific" – which just meant, that there were a lot of other Italian Catholic families on our street, we all attended the same church and frequented the same businesses.

When the family moved to Florida, the family neighborhoods were more eclectic in nature; meaning that I had exposure to many other cultures, creeds, and religions. I do not think I recognized the difference between being a "Believer" and "non-believer" when we first moved. I guess I just assumed everyone was a believer. (Not to quote a very popular "Monkee's" song).

My foundation of being a believer in God –whatever people call their "higher power" – gave me a peace and understanding that if I worked hard, "did good things", helped my fellow man, and adhering to the principles ("His will") I would have a good life.

In the Catholic religion there is a structure that is comforting. There are reasons and seasons for prayers, sacrament, and teachings. These are the basic social teachings from Pope(s) Leo XIII to FrancisAp:

- Respect for the human person
- Promotion of the family
- Right to own property
- The common good
- Subsidiarity
- The dignity of work and workers
- Pursuit of peace

- Care for the poor.

In all things, a belief in some "Higher Power," or "rules to live by" are important to create a foundation for you as a person; for how you interact with others; how you raise your family; and how you operate in business. That belief certainly worked for me and my family.

So, who or what do you believe in that you are able to gain strength, direction, and guidance from?

I am not trying to change anyone's opinions, or force religion on anyone. I am just simply stating that when people and organizations have foundations of belief; it builds confidence and structure for your team to flourish. (And remember, when I say TEAM, I mean a work team, a family or any group with a common thread or goal)

For you, personally; where do you gain your strength? What are your governing values? What do you believe in?

Do you notice a difference in people; in managers; in families that are believers? What are some of the common threads?

Governed by Different rules of life (they have rules)

A believer puts his faith, all his hope and trust in the person of God; a non-believer puts trust in himself; in society; or fruitless philosophies of man-made religion.

Believers know WE are the very temple of God. How we treat our bodies and each other is paramount

I say all of this, and point this out to share a very intimate thought about my belief structure. It begins with the Nicene Creed prayer:

"We believe in one God, the Father, the Almighty, Maker of heaven and earth, of all that is seen and unseen. We believe in one Lord Jesus Christ, the only Son of God, eternally begotten of the Father; God from God, Light from Light, true God from true God; begotten not made, one in being with the Father.."

None of the success that we have is Ours. I truly believe that all the "stuff" that we acquire in this life – and I say "stuff" to encompass the material, spiritual and emotional baggage (good connotation, not 'bad baggage') that we get to use while we are here on earth.

For lack of a better phrase, I believe all the good fortune that we have is "on loan" from God; and it is our duty to be responsible, creative, and multiply the good fortune we have through others.

By stating that – that all the good fortune is on loan – you may ask what I think about the "not so good" fortune?

I believe when unfortunate things happen there is a reason for it. I believe that we can learn lessons through the mistakes that we make; I believe that we can learn about ourselves when we are challenged and we are put in situations that we can handle – it is our ability to see through challenging situations that can reinforce our faith.

To sum up this portion; I believe in myself, I believe in my faith in God; I believe in the teachings of the Christian Faith and through those teachings I believe in others too – sometimes more than they believe in themselves.

I believe in the power of prayer. And because I believe in God and always put things in his hands, I have never wanted for anything. Through my strong faith, it helps me live a peaceful and complete life. .

The big question is …. DO YOU BELIEVE?

What about believing in people that do not believe in themselves? This book is really a self-evaluation book. How are you handling yourself and your affairs; your emotions; your personal time, your energy.

YOU are the first line of whether delegation to others is an EASY or HARD task. If you are not "right", your people who are relying on you for direction and vision will not be convinced of your good intentions.

In the ART of Delegation – the Attitude, Responsibility and Trust are paramount in delegation.

Believe in others

Believing in others would be the next step in the Delegation magic. There are a few points in this section that I would like to make sure you are looking for while you read this.

First, I am not saying that you should "blindly" trust or believe in anyone. I had a co-worker once that had a statement "Inspect what you Expect" – I always loved that saying. What it means, basically, is have "check points" to make sure the "project' is going the way it should.

Second, mistakes happen. Communication can be challenging in some situations. Just because someone makes a mistake, does not mean that they should lose your belief in them. People are still people and your reaction to "spilled milk" could jeopardize the way people feel about your intentions.

Lastly, reward wins. I truly believe that 60%, let's just say "more than half" of all success is in attitude. I can teach people skills to complete things; I can organize groups to rally around a problem; however, I cannot teach attitude.

At some point in an earlier chapter, I made a statement about making decisions quickly. I may have even referred to decision making as "swift and immediate" in matters of group dynamics. When workers, co-workers, team mates have a bad attitude, it will become a "cancer" of sorts throughout your organization.

Here is the twist in the plot. When you believe in yourself and it comes from a good place, you have a natural ability to believe in others. Conversely, when you believe in others that do not believe in themselves, you are fighting a losing battle.

Believe in the Process

What processes do you believe in? Throughout these chapters, I have given you action items; my challenges and facts about each of the topics. If you do not believe that through thoughtful action items and practice you can improve your managerial, delegation and process skills; this read was all for naught.

However, if you believe that The ART of Delegation begins with you, you will have the best success with implementing your plan.

From a process standpoint; anything you would like to improve upon will depend on your learning style and the way you adopt new ways of doing things. Some people read, like you are doing now; some people process only by actually doing the process over and over until they get it "right"; others are better at mimicking or replicating what others successes have been.

By the way, this is a good time to remind you that people watch all the time. Your co-workers, team mates, employees are all watching you and they could be learning from your actions on how to behave, speak, conquer the day. The people that learn by watching others are going to give you a lesson in yourself.

Getting back to trusting the process. When you implement a process for your organization, make sure you stick to it – even if there are challenges with it. Work through the challenges, do not scrap the whole process. Does that make sense? It is the old adage, "do not throw the baby out with the bath water". New processes will always have flaws. In fact, I remember one supervisor I had that used to say "the first draft of anything is shit".

I learned from that.

Treat all new processes as a draft. Make it known that the new process is a draft. Alert all involved that you will be asking them for feedback as you go through the process for improvements in execution, delivery or outcome.

Can you see how this approach would be more effective for the team. They are watching "the process" with a different eye; they are executing the process with a little more care and consideration to find the flaws; and they expecting that things will change as a result of their input.

Now, you have a mutually respectful – "I believe in you" foundation for anything new that may challenge the "change acceleration process" – (that could be the next book!).

Back to how all this believing is important to The ART of Delegation. Mutually beneficial relationships are built on ART; it could be the ART of anything.

ATTITUDE, RESPONSIBILITY AND TRUST

As a CEO of several companies, I know how challenging things can be, in general. Once I learned the tactics of the ART of Delegation (mostly through trials and tribulations); suddenly, "things" changed for me, and changed for those around me.

The most impactful part of my CEO-ship has been the relationships I have improved. First and foremost, my relationship with myself, God and my family has prospered greatly! Seriously, I don't worry about anything because I believe in myself. I believe in my family and my friends that I surround myself with.

I believe in the people that work for our organizations. I believe that they wake up every day with the intention of a good day's work, a productive outcome for the organization, and fostering relationships for future endeavors.

I believe in the processes of change for the better. As the CEO, it is my responsibility to continue to grow the organization for the betterment of the community, the future of the employees and to keep up with the ever-changing markets.

What about you? What do you need to do to adopt this way of thinking? Believing in others is tough these days when no one seems trustworthy.

Believe in yourself. Build the trust with your co-workers to allow great things to flourish and multiply.

I have a personal story, that seems to fit here. I think I have shared throughout the book that I am not perfect. I have challenges just like everyone. My approach to those challenges has changed over the years as I have grown.

This story is not one that has an ending because I am still working on the solutions. It is one that many CEOs and Managers may share and a solution may be provided, or considered by the end of the story.

I have been called un-approachable.

You may be thinking, You? Yes, Me. Let me tell you more of the story.

I request and honor feedback from my employees. My most valued employees tell me the things I do not always want to hear. Especially things like "you are unapproachable".

It is all very confusing to me. I am going to refer to "They" as the people in my organization. Unfortunately, I do not have the same relationship with everyone in the organization. Some "they's" have reached out and I have spent time coaching, listening, and helping them form their solutions. Other "they's" I know by name, and maybe some details of their history.

How could "they" call me unapproachable?

I have a good attitude when I come in to the office. I make eye contact. I listen, when asked. When people have a problem "they" cannot solve, I give my best processes of coming up with a solution.

I'm not dispelling what people feel. In fact, this is one of

94

the only questions that I have not been able to answer or fix. What is it about me that people find unapproachable?

I believe in everyone, until they give me a reason not to. In which case, most likely they will find another place to be – not in my organization.

I think I point this out here because sometimes there is no reason why someone gives you a label. Some labels are given based on "their" interpretation of how you handled yourself or any situation. Some labels are given because it is a projection of others challenges.

Maybe I will never get the answer to this "unapproachable" label, but what I can tell you is this. I will not stop being the person that I am because of a label without a reason.

Here is another plot twist to this – I have been told as a result of my questioning – I am not vocal enough in our sales meetings. My team wanted to "take over" the sales meetings as a stretch assignment for them. Sheesh! What about that makes me "unapproachable?"

How much of this label has anything to do with my actions or inactions? I cannot remember a time I ever "blew anyone off", or didn't make time for a conversation. And why should I even let it rent any space in my head?

Because I care, that's why. And part of the nuance of The ART of Delegation is much more about improving relationships and outcomes; than it is about being able to "tell people what to do".

Bottom line is, continue to believe in yourself and do things with the best intentions. Continue to push people to their greatest limits to exercise their abilities to soar and achieve their greatest accomplishments. Do not let the opinions of others interfere the destiny of your successes.

Of the thousands of people that I have employed, how many said I was unapproachable? Eh, does it really matter?

I'll keep asking for feedback. Meanwhile, let us move on to some action items and thoughts.

Action items:

- Identify what your governing principles are – believe in something bigger than yourself.

- Take the time to connect with people and allow them to experience believing in themselves. Give a task – reward and recognize OR give a task – teach – give feedback – reward and recognize their contribution.

- Make sure the organization has clearly mapped out

  processes for "normal" business practices, like hiring, for instance. On boarding new employees; training provided for new skills etc.

- Whatever processes, whatever people you have trust them; coach them, challenge them.

My challenges:

- I think we covered my big challenge. When others have labels for you, it could be simply that they do not believe in themselves. Projection is a real thing.

- I guess my challenge is learning when to "let a label go". I will not spend much time on it, but every time the "unapproachable" tag comes up, I want to make sure I am doing my due diligence to identify something I could be doing better. (by the way, this is also in some small part, the definition of emotional intelligence – understanding that you do not have to take things personally)

Facts when people Believe and are believed in their/they/they are:

- Fear decreases
- Confidence increases
- Bravery to aim higher and take a leap of faith
- Feel Supported
- Focus increases
- Increase in productivity
- Positive thinking is infectious
- People admit mistakes
- Handle conflict gracefully

- Language is better (no foul language)
- Punctuality is consistent

For all intents and purposes, you could say that when you believe in yourself and in others you hold the magic recipe, the foundation, of The ART of Delegation.

Arguably, when you see changes in confidence and fear, punctuality, or language; that may be a time to check in.

As a part of this series, the ART is truly in your commitment to change and identify areas of opportunity for your success to flourish in any environment. Whether you are looking for ways to improve your relationships or your trajectory of business success; you have the power within you to do that.

All change can only begin with you.

A Quick Story:
:

This chapter is dedicated to my amazing and gorgeous wife Laura. She has taught me to believe in myself and that things will always work out for the better.

Her strong faith in God and ability to let things go, has provided me the opportunity to take risks, to never worry, while providing a certain level of inner peace within our family.

The word "Believe" has many facets to it. For me, it is a sense of internal freedom that a I possess in order to let my mind wander to manifest something to happen. Then I figure out the path to take.

It was the summer of 2009 we were broke , the economy was in the shitter and very few sales in real estate, there was no light at the end of what appeared to be a dark tunnel.

I recall going to Lowes to get an A/C filter for the house and I saw 3 realtors I knew working there as employees.

When I got home, I said to my wife, I think it is a sign maybe I should get a job at Lowe's to supplement my income while the real estate market is slow. She said "Don't be silly John, you're not going to work at Lowes, you're an amazing business owner and salesman stop being stupid and figure it out".

Later on that week I created a marketing program for our real estate business: "I'll sell your home in 99 days or my Commission will be Free!"

I immediately put that marketing plan into action and started getting listings again which in turn also attracted buyers.

Overnight I was back making money again, meeting new homeowners, which new energy and a purpose again that I had been missing.

I got the kick in the ass that I needed; we all need sometimes from our greatest people. Thank you, Laura, for always keeping me grounded and out of "blue vests". Thank you for reminding me that we have the talent and ability to do anything.

I also believe in the power of prayer. And when we put things in God's hands and believe in him, all things.

10 PUTTING "IT" ALL TOGETHER

Ask Yourself these questions.

What did you think this book was going to be about?
What changes are you willing to make?
Is Delegation important to you?

I suppose the most important questions in this book is What will happen when you delegate more effectively? How much more do you think your organization will accomplish? How much better will retention be in the organization?

Maybe a better question is what you are willing to do to make a difference in your management style. This book is all about improving your management style by improving skills that will make you a better communicator, achieve higher understanding and allowing you to do and focus on the things you are great at and LOVE TO DO!

101

When you are focused on the "end game", the goals and the team, your ability to focus on your best contributions happen. By the way, when you let people do what they are good at; what they love to do, you are promoting growth, confidence and possibly greater achievements for others as well.

Bottom line is, human equity is the most treasured asset in any organization. When you take the time to invest in yourself, like you have done in purchasing this book; and investing the time, like you have taken to evaluate your skills as it relates to:

Listening more effectively
Believing in yourself and the processes
Empowering others
Taking time for yourself
Trusting your gut
Taking the time to vision, plan, and share

You are well on your way of mastering the **ART of Delegation.**

Most management books talk about theory and how the Author may help the reader acknowledge behaviors in others. I have found the most challenging and rewarding skills have resulted from my self-awareness; and my constant drive for improvement in everything I do.

The ART of Delegation is mastering our own skills in People management. Guess what? understanding what motivates others is a true gift and requires Attitude, Responsibility and Trust to develop this gift in all the right ways.

Delegation, essentially, is like any other "engine" that needs fuel, energy, attention, and maintenance. It requires monitoring of performance and skill. It takes a great attitude, respect and responsibility and Trust to fuel that engine.

How do you know if you are delegating effectively? That is a great question! There will be tell-tale signs about your delegation success. One important sign is the retention and energy of the team. When people are excited about a project or a goal, it shows. Team mates will often stay late, they are more punctual, reliable and dependable.

What are some other attributes of a team to know you are delegating effectively? Well, if you are in a sales business – people who are excited about their contribution sell more; if in a production business – people produce more and better quality products; you get the picture.

Lastly, and most likely the most challenging for a manager is the fact that when you delegate effectively, the team contributes more – promotions happen, new employees need to be on boarded, and the process of grooming, mentoring, and delegating continues.

I have always loved the nature of team work and the functions of business acumen. I realized a long time ago; I did not need to be good at everything. I just wanted to do the things I loved to do – hence, the title of the book "The Art of Delegation: Do what you love to do".

I am extremely capable of doing many things. The best thing I learned is how to get things done through people. By me concentrating on the vision and the plan (the thing I love to do); I was creating confidence in others. Through delegation, I was not only creating a business; I was helping people gain skill and purpose.

If you have never created a team before. Start now. Teams can be created through collaboration, confidence, a little competition, and care. Start at home, or in your circle of friends, or in the workplace. Surprise yourself.

How to start? Well, in order to delegate effectively, you need a plan. The plan can be for anything! As simple as, what meal to make for dinner or as complex as expanding a product line. Once you have the plan, the real work begins.

I have created a work book, a simple add on to this book, to help you with delegating anything and improving the lives of others. You will discover in the work book a simple start to creating a plan and delegating to the correct people.

Putting it all together is simple for me. I have some "go to" actions that have been sprinkled throughout this book. These skills help in delegation, coordination, and participation.

Improve your Conversations:

- I ask more questions, rather than respond.
- I always keep others' perspectives in mind

- I am respectful in realizing that everyone has a perspective
- I listen fully without judgement, or needing to respond.
- I try to understand what the outcome of the conversation is going to be– does this person need advice? Instruction? Motivation? Or just someone to listen? – and ask for clarification, if need be.

When delegating to others:
- I make sure everyone understands the vision and the plan
- I make sure that everyone has an opportunity to ask for instruction or ask for a resource
- I have check-ins; it may not be ME checking in, but the system and process is in place to make sure we stay on timelines.
- I refocus, give feedback, reward, and recognize the organization in timely fashion at checkpoints.

For myself:
- I have regularly scheduled personal time so that I can recharge and reevaluate progress.
- I have learned to trust my gut and pull the "proverbial trigger" on good ideas, bad ideas and important decisions
- I believe. I believe in myself. I believe in the great people that I am blessed to be surrounded with
- I am thankful and grateful for the positive foundation that gave me the footing for all that I can do; for my family who supports all our endeavors

and for the people, employees, colleagues, and friends who always show up when the "going gets tough".

As a final thought about "giving life all you've got;" remember that when you delegate you are fulfilling others' dreams of being a part of something bigger than themselves. Delegation allows others to grow, to stretch themselves; and it also allows YOU, the "delegator" to grow in many ways.

Give your organization, your family, and your friends that best YOU – the you that helps foster relationships, wealth, literacy, acumen and to help people dream bigger than they ever thought they could.

Delegate – make it an ART. Focus on what you love to do!

ABOUT THE AUTHOR

I was born in Utica, New York; raised as a typical Italian-American kid, eating pasta, making homemade pizzas, and attending Catholic school.

My parents moved our family to central Florida when I was 11 years old and when we arrived, they started encouraging me in different ways. In exchange for allowance for chores, they paid me to read "self-help" books. This really seemed to spark my motivation, not just because of the content, simply to read more.

At 22 years old, in May of 1998, I was working at AT&T Wireless (and skipping college). I was made aware of a void in the cellular business when corporations let all their repair technicians go, and moved the direction of customer service to a centralized "mail in your phone for service" model.

After seeing the pitfalls in this model, customers without

their phones for a week and the poor customer service that occurred because of this change; I met someone that changed my trajectory.

At one of my shifts at AT&T, this gentleman helped me learn how to do light repairs on phones which quickly segued into creating a business model around making your phone "fashionable."

Tired of working out of my car after a month, I opened the first "repair and fashion cell phone" kiosk in the local mall and turned it quickly into a profitable business. Quickly realizing that making money and working for myself was fun; it would be so much more fun doing it with my friends.so that we could all hang out and travel together and enjoy our best lives all on an even playing field. After mastering my second location I decided to turn the company into a business opportunity for others to join in and licensed the company name as "Wireless Dimensions;" The opportunity and the products became a business in a box.

This opportunity grew into 156 mall locations in 38 states in just 4.5 years.

I later sold the company to a large investment company and entered the wonderful world of Real Estate.

I have two adult children, now in college, Gianni, and Nadia. I have been married to my amazing wife Laura for 23 Years.

I have decided to share my knowledge of life and business with people. It is time. We are empty-nesters now, and I feel the need to share information to help people that need a direction, or an inspiring story, or just some foundational business acumen.

I love to travel abroad and all around the United States in my RV. I am also an avid tennis player and enjoy the warm waters of Florida exploring on my Seadoo.

My favorite motto? "Just Do It" by Nike ®

Get in Touch!

STAY IN TOUCH!

As a part of this book, you can Download the workbook for Free, by just putting in your email address. We will only let you know when other books are available and you can unsubscribe at any time. Scan the barcode and let's get down to the ART of Business!

Visit JohnCurriART.com

www.ingramcontent.com/pod-product-compliance
Lightning Source LLC
Chambersburg PA
CBHW062329290526
45794CB00005B/1959